www.providencebooks.net

Publisher Contact

Email:contact@providencebooks.net

Social media: facebook.com/providencebooks

Acknowledgements

The team at Providence Books would like to thank our friends, family, suppliers and customers for making our vision of creating the highest-quality books a reality. Thanks for purchasing and enjoy the quotes!

This page is intentionally left blank

This page is intentionally left blank

'Social engineering,' the fancy term for tricking you into giving away your digital secrets, is at least as great a threat as spooky technology.

Barton Gellman

A minimum precaution: keep your anti-malware protections up to date, and install security updates for all your software as soon as they arrive.

Barton Gellman

A national security letter cannot be used to authorize eavesdropping or to read the contents of e-mail. But it does permit investigators to trace revealing paths through the private affairs of a modern digital citizen.

Barton Gellman

Activists and geeks, standing together, are demonstrating powers beyond the reach of government control.

Barton Gellman

Al Qaeda is closely aligned with the Chechens.

Barton Gellman

All Americans are dependent for their energy on the Arabian peninsula.

Barton Gellman

Among all the upheavals of war with al Qaeda, the surest indicator of the historic stakes is the ongoing rotation of top U.S. government managers - scores at a time - into a bunker deep underground and far from Washington.

Barton Gellman

As Trotsky didn't exactly say, you may not be interested in electronic snoops, but snoops are interested in you, whether or not you keep Coke's secret recipe on your iPhone.

Barton Gellman

As digital communications have multiplied, and NSA capabilities with them, the agency has shifted resources from surveillance of individual targets to the acquisition of communications on a planetary scale.

Barton Gellman

As militias go, the Ohio Defense Force is on the moderate side.

Barton Gellman

At Cheney's initiative, the United States stripped terror suspects of long-established rights under domestic and international law, building a new legal edifice under exclusive White House ownership.

Barton Gellman

At the height of Iraq's clandestine nuclear weapons program, which nearly succeeded in building a bomb in 1991, Tuwaitha incorporated research reactors, uranium mining and enrichment facilities, chemical engineering plants and an explosives fabrication center to build the device that detonates a nuclear core.

Barton Gellman

By now, you've heard endless warnings about the risk of short, trivial passwords. There's a good chance you ignore them.

Barton Gellman

Cheney was among the best secretaries of defence the country has ever had. He was a very effective White House chief of staff. He did not make many enemies, and he had the ability to persuade people with that soft tone and very reasonable style of his. He's always been exceptionally good as the right-hand man.

Barton Gellman

China and Russia are regarded as the most formidable cyber threats.

Barton Gellman

Clinton saw himself much more as the steward of alliances and of consensus that moved in the right direction. He didn't see himself as someone who could change the overall thrust, I think, of global policy.

Barton Gellman

Cloud services cut both ways in terms of security: you get off-site backup and disaster recovery, but you entrust your secrets to somebody else's hands. Doing the latter increases your exposure to government surveillance and the potential for deliberate or inadvertent breaches of your confidential files.

Barton Gellman

CloudShield did not see itself as a cloak-and-dagger company. It made its name for high-end hardware that could peer deeply into Internet traffic and pull out and analyze 'packets' of data as they flew by.

Barton Gellman

Companies that receive government information demands have to obey the law, but they often have room for maneuver. They scarcely ever use it.

Barton Gellman

Counterterrorism analysts have known for years that al Qaeda prepares for attacks with elaborate 'targeting packages' of photographs and notes.

Barton Gellman

Daniel Ellsberg showed tremendous courage back in the '70s.

Barton Gellman

Dell fills its computers with crapware, collecting fees from McAfee and other vendors to pre-install 'trial' versions.

Barton Gellman

Doctrines don't govern policy. They provide a conceptual framework by which policymakers approach their decisions. But there is no such thing as a doctrine that controls policy in every way.

Barton Gellman

Drug manufacturers could afford to sell AIDS drugs in Africa at virtually any discount. The companies said they did not do so because Africa lacked the requisite infrastructure.

Barton Gellman

During the morning rush hour on March 20, 1995, the Japanese cult Aum Shinrikyo placed packages on five subway trains converging on Tokyo's central station. When punctured, the packages spread vaporized Sarin through the subway cars and then into the stations as the trains pulled in.

Barton Gellman

Early in 1986, the World Health Organization in Geneva still regarded AIDS as an ailment of the promiscuous few.

Barton Gellman

Ecuador has never stated flatly that it would give asylum to Edward Snowden.

Barton Gellman

Enclosed by a sand berm four miles around and 160 feet high, the Baghdad Nuclear Research Facility entombs what remains of reactors bombed by Israel in 1981 and the United States in 1991. It has stored industrial and medical wastes, along with spent reactor fuel.

Barton Gellman

Even complex passwords are getting easy to break if they're too short. That's because today's inexpensive computer chips have the power of supercomputers from the year 2000.

Barton Gellman

Everyone and his Big Brother wants to log your browsing habits, the better to build a profile of who you are and how you live your life - online and off. Search engine companies offer a benefit in return: more relevant search results. The more they know about you, the better they can tailor information to your needs.

Barton Gellman

Experts said public companies worry about the loss of customer confidence and the legal liability to shareholders or security vendors when they report flaws.

Barton Gellman

Federal prosecutors want to indict Julian Assange for making public a great many classified documents.

Barton Gellman

First developed as a weapon by the U.S. Army, VX is an oily, odorless and tasteless liquid that kills on contact with the skin or when inhaled in aerosol form. Like other nerve agents, it is treatable in the first minutes after exposure but otherwise leads swiftly to fatal convulsions and respiratory failure.

Barton Gellman

For a decade, makers of AIDS medicines had rejected the idea of lowering prices in poor countries for fear of eroding profits in rich ones. The position required a balancing act, because the companies had to deflect attacks on the global reach of their patents, which granted exclusive marketing rights for antiretroviral drugs.

Barton Gellman

For months, Obama administration officials attacked Snowden's motives and said the work of the NSA was distorted by selective leaks and misinterpretations.

Barton Gellman

For personal use, I recommend the free and open-source Truecrypt, which comes in flavors for Windows, Mac and Linux.

Barton Gellman

For political and bureaucratic reasons, governments at all levels are telling far less to the public than to insiders about how to prepare for and behave in the initial chaos of a mass-casualty event.

Barton Gellman

Friend of mine, a smart journalist, had his iPad stolen. He couldn't help that - the thief broke into his house. But his private, personal data wasn't stolen, exactly. Donated, more like. He had no passcode set on the iPad.

Barton Gellman

Ghostery lets you spy on the spies in your computer. For each web page you visit, this extension uncloaks some - but not all - of the invisible tracking software that is working behind the scenes.

Barton Gellman

Given the volume of PC sales and the way McAfee runs its operation, I imagine there must be thousands of phantom subscribers - folks who signed up once upon a time and left the software behind two or three computers ago.

Barton Gellman

Google appears to be the worst of the major search engines from a privacy point of view; Ask.com, with AskEraser turned on, is among the best.

Barton Gellman

Governors normally have jurisdiction over public health emergencies, but a widespread biological attack would cross state boundaries.

Barton Gellman

Holding our own government to account for the use of its power is, in my view, the highest mission of a U.S. news organization.

Barton Gellman

I do read licenses, and they aggravate me, but a computer isn't much good without software. When I need a product, I hold my nose and click 'agree.'

Barton Gellman

I don't say I never use Facebook, but I often think about closing my account.

Barton Gellman

I don't think Cheney started off in 2000 with a burning desire to become vice-president. I think the prospect gradually became more appealing, and he goosed the process.

Barton Gellman

I doubt there's any government in the world that guides itself primarily by strategy or conceptual documents or worldview. Anybody who has the reins of power has to look at practical limitations and tradeoffs - the fact that you can focus at most on one or two things at a time, that resources are limited.

Barton Gellman

I favor pocket-sized hard drives that travel between home and office, syncing with computers on both ends.

Barton Gellman

I have no evidence of any relationship between IRS and NSA.

Barton Gellman

I learned the technology and tradecraft of electronic security in self defense, with a lot of expert help.

Barton Gellman

I'm a journalist and author. I make my living by finding things out and writing about them.

Barton Gellman

I've always shied away from online data storage. I don't even use my employers' network drives for anything sensitive. I want to control access myself.

Barton Gellman

If Iraq had succeeded in spray-drying anthrax spores to extend their life and lethality, that would have been among the most important secrets of its wide-ranging weapons program.

Barton Gellman

If you do write down your passwords, don't make it obvious which password corresponds to which account. Even better, write the passwords incorrectly and make up an easy rule for fixing them. You could decide to add 1 to each number in your password, so that 2x6Y is written as 3x7Y.

Barton Gellman

In 1995, Glaxo bought Burroughs Wellcome and became the presumptive leader in AIDS therapy.

Barton Gellman

In Africa through the 1990s, with notable exceptions in Senegal and Uganda, nearly all the ruling powers denied they had a problem with AIDS.

Barton Gellman

In computer circles, any unencrypted data is known as 'cleartext.'

Barton Gellman

In effect, you cannot stop Iraq from growing nasty bugs in the basement. You can stop them from putting operational warheads on working missiles and launching them at their neighbors.

Barton Gellman

In general, states do not count on pledges of 'no more war' from their neighbors. Israel's army never counted on it from Egypt, for example.

Barton Gellman

In late 2003, the Bush administration reversed a long-standing policy requiring agents to destroy their files on innocent American citizens, companies and residents when investigations closed.

Barton Gellman

In the field of biological weapons, there is almost no prospect of detecting a pathogen until it has been used in an attack.

Barton Gellman

In the urgent aftermath of Sept. 11, 2001, with more attacks thought to be imminent, analysts wanted to use 'contact chaining' techniques to build what the NSA describes as network graphs of people who represented potential threats.

Barton Gellman

In the wealthy industrialized nations, effective drug therapies against AIDS became available - AZT as early as 1987, then combinations of antiretroviral agents in 1996. The new drugs offered hope that fatal complications might be staved off and AIDS rendered a chronic condition.

Barton Gellman

Iraq has the most extensive petrochemical industry in the Middle East and a wealth of vaccine factories, single-cell protein research labs, medical and veterinary manufacturing centers and water treatment plants.

Barton Gellman

Iraq has, in effect, one export of any consequence. That's oil.

Barton Gellman

It no longer counts as remarkable that Egyptians organized their uprising on social media.

Barton Gellman

It turns out that American Express honors recurring payments even if the vendor is unable to supply an accurate card number and expiration date. An Amex phone representative said this is a feature, not a bug, which makes sure my bills are paid.

Barton Gellman

Leaders at the top of al Qaeda's hierarchy, the evidence shows, completed plans and obtained the materials required to manufacture two biological toxins - botulinum and salmonella - and the chemical poison cyanide.

Barton Gellman

Most computers today have built in backup software.

Barton Gellman

Most people inside the bureau believe that the blown opportunities to head off 9/11 would not recur today. Even among the FBI's doubters, few disagree that the bureau has come a long way.

Barton Gellman

NSA surveillance is a complex subject - legally, technically and operationally.

Barton Gellman

Nearly all government advice on terrorism sacrifices practical particulars for an unalarming tone. The usual guidance is to maintain a three-day supply of food and water along with a radio, flashlight, batteries and first-aid kit.

Barton Gellman

No one can keep track of how many people use Internet, how many machines it can reach, or even how many sub- and sub-sub-networks form a part of it.

Barton Gellman

No one ought to be under any illusion that Cheney privately thinks himself a failure.

Barton Gellman

NoScript is probably the most important privacy tool, but it costs you in convenience.

Barton Gellman

Nothing is absolute in security.

Barton Gellman

Obama's ascendancy unhinged the radical right, offering a unified target to competing camps of racial, nativist and religious animus.

Barton Gellman

Of all Iraq's rocket scientists, none drew warier scrutiny abroad than Modher Sadeq-Saba Tamimi.

Barton Gellman

On March 12, 2004, acting attorney general James B. Comey and the Justice Department's top leadership reached the brink of resignation over electronic surveillance orders that they believed to be illegal.

Barton Gellman

On average, since 9/11, the FBI reckons that just over 100,000 terrorism leads each year have come over the transom. Analysts and agents designate them as immediate, priority or routine, but the bureau says every one is covered.

Barton Gellman

One common puzzle for the security-minded is how to work with confidential data on the road. Sometimes you can't bring your laptop, or don't want to. But working on somebody else's machine exposes you to malware and leaves behind all kinds of electronic trails.

Barton Gellman

Ordinary Geiger counters, worn on belt clips and resembling pagers, have been in use by the U.S. Customs Service for years.

Barton Gellman

Pakistan has accepted some security training from the CIA, but U.S. export restrictions and Pakistani suspicions have prevented the two countries from sharing the most sophisticated technology for safeguarding nuclear components.

Barton Gellman

Pakistan has dozens of laboratories and production and storage sites scattered across the country. After developing warheads with highly enriched uranium, it has more recently tried to do the same with more-powerful and compact plutonium.

Barton Gellman

Palestinians have had to live for a long time with the fact that Israelis had power over them in their everyday lives.

Barton Gellman

Privacy and encryption work, but it's too easy to make a mistake that exposes you.

Barton Gellman

Privacy is relational. It depends on the audience. You don't want your employer to know you're job hunting. You don't spill all about your love life to your mom or your kids. You don't tell trade secrets to your rivals.

Barton Gellman

Rolf Ekeus, his appearance can deceive. He looks somewhere between an international diplomat and a mad professor. He's got that sort of shock of white hair and a slightly absent-minded way of speaking. But he's extremely sharp and very serious about power relationships.

Barton Gellman

Scores of armed antigovernment groups, some of them far more radical, have formed or been revived during the Obama years, according to law-enforcement agencies and outside watchdogs.

Barton Gellman

Scott Ritter is a very well-known archetype of a certain U.S. military officer. Very hard talking, very ambitious, zealous, and completely consumed with carrying out his mission. He's a guy who, throughout his career, I would say, did not break rules, but he worked around road blocks.

Barton Gellman

Searches of al Qaeda sites in Afghanistan, undertaken since American-backed forces took control there, are not known to have turned up a significant cache of nuclear materials.

Barton Gellman

Smallpox, which spreads by respiration and kills roughly one in three of those infected, took hundreds of millions of lives during a recorded history dating to Pharaonic Egypt. The last case was in 1978, and the disease was declared eradicated on May 8, 1980.

Barton Gellman

Snowden grants that NSA employees by and large believe in their mission and trust the agency to handle the secrets it takes from ordinary people - deliberately, in the case of bulk records collection, and 'incidentally,' when the content of American phone calls and e-mails are swept into NSA systems along with foreign targets.

Barton Gellman

Snowden has been very sparing about discussing his early life or his personal life.

Barton Gellman

Snowden has yet to tell me anything that was a fact that I have been able to rebut or that anybody in the U.S. government I have talked to has been able to rebut.

Barton Gellman

Snowden is an orderly thinker, with an engineer's approach to problem-solving.

Barton Gellman

Some misunderstandings are hard to cure.

Barton Gellman

Stuxnet, a computer worm reportedly developed by the United States and Israel that destroyed Iranian nuclear centrifuges in attacks in 2009 and 2010, is often cited as the most dramatic use of a cyber weapon.

Barton Gellman

Sudan expelled bin Laden on May 18, 1996, to Afghanistan.

Barton Gellman

Suppose a bad guy guesses the password for your throwaway Yahoo address. Now he goes to major banking and commerce sites and looks for an account registered to that email address. When he finds one, he clicks the 'forgot my password' button and a new one is sent - to your compromised email account. Now he's in a position to do you serious harm.

Barton Gellman

The $52.6 billion U.S. intelligence arsenal is aimed mainly at unambiguous adversaries, including al-Qaida, North Korea and Iran. But top-secret budget documents reveal an equally intense focus on one purported ally: Pakistan.

Barton Gellman

The CIA now assesses that four nations - Iraq, North Korea, Russia and, to the surprise of some specialists, France - have undeclared samples of the smallpox virus.

Barton Gellman

The IronClad is faster than most thumb drives but far slower than a standard hard drive. Boot up, application launch and other Windows operations feel sluggish, though still usable.

Barton Gellman

The NSA has different reporting requirements for each branch of government and each of its legal authorities.

Barton Gellman

The NSA is forbidden to 'target' American citizens, green-card holders or companies for surveillance without an individual warrant from a judge.

Barton Gellman

The NSA's business is 'information dominance,' the use of other people's secrets to shape events.

Barton Gellman

The National Security Agency has broken privacy rules or overstepped its legal authority thousands of times each year since Congress granted the agency broad new powers in 2008, according to an internal audit and other top-secret documents.

Barton Gellman

The Obama administration has provided almost no public information about the NSA's compliance record.

Barton Gellman

The Obama administration, like those before it, promotes a disturbingly narrow interpretation of the Fourth Amendment, misapplying the facts of old analog cases to a radically different digital world.

Barton Gellman

The Patriot Act unleashed the FBI to search your email, travel and credit records without even a suspicion of wrongdoing.

Barton Gellman

The U.N. Security Council ordered Iraq in April 1991 to relinquish all capabilities to make biological, chemical and nuclear weapons as well as long-range missiles.

Barton Gellman

The U.S. government has known since the early 1990s about Soviet-era smallpox weapons, and collected circumstantial evidence of programs elsewhere.

Barton Gellman

The United States, a signatory to the Chemical Weapons Convention, destroyed the last of its stocks of VX and other chemical agents on the Johnston Atoll, 825 miles southwest of Hawaii, in November 2000.

Barton Gellman

The best way to preserve your privacy is to use a search engine that does not keep your logs in the first place. That's the approach used by Startpage and its European parent company, Ixquick.

Barton Gellman

The causes and severity of NSA infractions vary widely. One in 10 incidents is attributed to a typographical error in which an analyst enters an incorrect query and retrieves data about U.S phone calls or emails.

Barton Gellman

The defection of Hussein Kamel was a turning point in the U.N.-imposed disarmament of Iraq in the 1990s.

Barton Gellman

The federal government is often said in militia circles to have made wholesale seizures of power, at times by subterfuge. A leading grievance holds that the 16th Amendment, which authorizes the federal income tax, was ratified through fraud.

Barton Gellman

The first and pivotal negotiations over global access to AIDS drugs began in Geneva in 1991. They lasted two years, but confidential minutes suggest they were doomed the first day.

Barton Gellman

The first reports of AIDS closely followed the inauguration of President Ronald Reagan, whose 'family values' agenda and alliance with Christian conservatives associated AIDS with deviance and sin.

Barton Gellman

The first time I set out to find George F. Kennan, in 1982, I had just turned 21, begun my final semester at Princeton University and noticed with astonishment that the senior thesis deadline had crept to within four months.

Barton Gellman

The funny thing is that Dick Cheney has done more than anybody in the White House for quite a long time to throw up roadblocks against future historians.

Barton Gellman

The government of Sudan, employing a back channel direct from its president to the Central Intelligence Agency, offered in the early spring of 1996 to arrest Osama bin Laden and place him in Saudi custody, according to officials and former officials in all three countries.

Barton Gellman

The gravest risks from al Qaeda combine its affinity for big targets and its announced desire for weapons of mass destruction.

Barton Gellman

The modern era of continuity planning began under President Ronald Reagan.

Barton Gellman

The surveillance of ordinary people is far greater than I would have imagined and far greater than the American public has been able to debate.

Barton Gellman

There is evidence that some of al Qaeda's nuclear efforts over the years met with swindles and false leads.

Barton Gellman

There is no reliable way to calculate from the number of recorded compliance issues how many Americans have had their communications improperly collected, stored or distributed by the NSA.

Barton Gellman

There's a long history of private-company cooperation with the NSA that dates back to at least the 1970s.

Barton Gellman

Throughout the early and mid-1990s, the Clinton administration debated the merits of paying for AIDS testing and counseling of vulnerable populations overseas.

Barton Gellman

True net-heads sometimes resort to punctuation cartoons to get around the absence of inflection.

Barton Gellman

U.S. intelligence services routinely use collection methods against foreigners that foreseeably - with certainty - ingest high volumes of U.S. communications as well.

Barton Gellman

U.S. surveillance of Pakistan extends far beyond its nuclear program. There are several references in the black budget to expanding U.S. scrutiny of chemical and biological laboratories.

Barton Gellman

Unsettling signs of al Qaeda's aims and skills in cyberspace have led some government experts to conclude that terrorists are at the threshold of using the Internet as a direct instrument of bloodshed.

Barton Gellman

We know what's in our Cheerios and in our retirement accounts because the law requires disclosure.

Barton Gellman

Well-secured files don't do you much good if you lose them in a fire or hard drive crash.

Barton Gellman

When the 'New York Times' revealed the warrantless surveillance of voice calls, in December 2005, the telephone companies got nervous.

Barton Gellman

White House officials acknowledge in broad terms that a president's time and public rhetoric are among his most valuable policy tools.

Barton Gellman

Why does it appear that interested readers so often attribute flaws to 'the press' rather than taking particular issue with particular reports?

Barton Gellman

You don't need to be a spook to care about encryption. If you travel with your computer or keep it in a place where other people can put their hands on it, you're vulnerable.

Barton Gellman

This page is intentionally left blank

This page is intentionally left blank

This page is intentionally left blank

This page is intentionally left blank

This page is intentionally left blank

www.ingramcontent.com/pod-product-compliance
Lightning Source LLC
Chambersburg PA
CBHW071152280526
45787CB00003B/1493